Keep this pocket-sized
you are visiting Blackp
in the locality.

Whether you are in your car or on foot, you will
enjoy an evocative journey back in time. Compare
the Blackpool of old with what you can see
today—see how the streets, parks and open spaces
have changed; examine the shops and buildings and
notice how they have been altered
or replaced; look at fine details such as lamp-posts,
shop fascias and trade signs; and see the many
alterations to Blackpool and its surrounding area that
have taken place unnoticed during our lives, some of
which we may have taken for granted.

At the turn of a page you will gain fascinating
insights into Blackpool's unique history.

FRANCIS FRITH'S
pocket ALBUM

BLACKPOOL

A POCKET ALBUM

Adapted from an original book by
CLIVE HARDY

First published in the United Kingdom in 2005 by
Frith Book Company Ltd

ISBN 1-84589-076-0
Text and Design copyright © Frith Book Company Ltd
Photographs copyright © The Francis Frith Collection

The Frith photographs and the Frith logo are reproduced under licence from Heritage
Photographic Resources Ltd, the owners of the Frith archive and trademarks

British Library Cataloguing in Publication Data

Blackpool—A Pocket Album
Adapted from an original book by Clive Hardy

Frith Book Company Ltd
Frith's Barn, Teffont,
Salisbury, Wiltshire SP3 5QP
Tel: +44 (0) 1722 716 376
Email: info@francisfrith.co.uk
www.francisfrith.co.uk

Printed and bound in Great Britain by MPG, Bodmin

Front Cover: **BLACKPOOL, FROM NORTH PIER 1906** 53853t
The colour-tinting is for illustrative purposes only, and is not intended to be historically accurate.

Frontispiece: **BLACKPOOL, THE PROMENADE 1890** 22875

AS WITH ANY HISTORICAL DATABASE THE FRITH ARCHIVE IS CONSTANTLY
BEING CORRECTED AND IMPROVED AND THE PUBLISHERS WOULD WELCOME
INFORMATION ON OMISSIONS OR INACCURACIES

CONTENTS

FRANCIS FRITH
VICTORIAN PIONEER

Francis Frith, founder of the world-famous photographic archive, was a complex and multi-talented man. A devout Quaker and a highly successful Victorian businessman, he was philosophic by nature and pioneering in outlook. By 1855 he had already established a wholesale grocery business in Liverpool, and sold it for the astonishing sum of £200,000, which is the equivalent today of over £15,000,000. Now in his thirties, and captivated by the new science of photography, Frith set out on a series of pioneering journeys up the Nile and to the Near East.

INTRIGUE AND EXPLORATION

He was the first photographer to venture beyond the sixth cataract of the Nile. Africa was still the mysterious 'Dark Continent', and Stanley and Livingstone's historic meeting was a decade into the future. The conditions for picture taking confound belief. He laboured for hours in his wicker dark-room in the sweltering heat of the desert, while the volatile chemicals fizzed dangerously in their trays. Back in London he exhibited his photographs and was 'rapturously cheered' by members of the Royal Society. His reputation as a photographer was made overnight.

VENTURE OF A LIFE-TIME

By the 1870s the railways had threaded their way across the country, and Bank Holidays and half-day Saturdays had been made obligatory by Act of Parliament. All of a sudden the working man and his family were able to enjoy days out, take holidays, and see a little more of the world.

With typical business acumen, Francis Frith foresaw that these new tourists would enjoy having souvenirs to commemorate their days out. For the next thirty years he travelled the country by train and by pony and trap, producing fine photographs of seaside resorts and beauty spots that were keenly bought by millions of Victorians. These prints were painstakingly pasted into family albums and pored over during the dark nights of winter, rekindling precious memories of summer excursions. Frith's studio was soon supplying retail shops all over the country, and by 1890 F Frith & Co had become the greatest specialist photographic publishing company in the world, with over 2,000 sales outlets, and pioneered the picture postcard.

FRANCIS FRITH'S LEGACY

Francis Frith had died in 1898 at his villa in Cannes, his great project still growing. The archive he created continued in business for another seventy years. By 1970 it contained over a third of a million pictures showing 7,000 British towns and villages.

Frith's legacy to us today is of immense significance and value, for the magnificent archive of evocative photographs he created provides a unique record of change in the cities, towns and villages throughout Britain over a century and more. Frith and his fellow studio photographers revisited locations many times down the years to update their views, compiling for us an enthralling and colourful pageant of British life and character.

We are fortunate that Frith was dedicated to recording the minutiae of everyday life. For it is this sheer wealth of visual data, the painstaking chronicle of changes in dress, transport, street layouts, buildings, housing, engineering and landscape that captivates us so much today, offering us a powerful link with the past and with the lives of our ancestors.

Computers have now made it possible for Frith's many thousands of images to be accessed almost instantly. The archive offers every one of us an opportunity to examine the places where we and our families have lived and worked down the years. Its images, depicting our shared past, are now bringing pleasure and enlightenment to millions around the world a century and more after his death.

BLACKPOOL
AN INTRODUCTION

THE EARLY YEARS

The first reference to Blackpool that we have with any certainty appears in the Bispham Church register for 1602, recording the christening of 'Ellen Cowban, daughter of Thomas Cowban of blackpoole'. And that is precisely what the place was; a black pool, near the mouth of the Spen, its waters coloured by the peaty moss through which it flowed. The area was remote, marshy and windswept, and was a part of Lancashire known as Agmunderness, whose main townships included Poulton, Rossall, Bispham, Lytham, Thornton and Inskip. When Ellen was alive, most people along this part of the coast lived in single-storey cottages built with arched timbers (crooks), wattle and clay walls, and thatch made from rushes.

One of the first houses of any substance to be built near the black pool was Fox Hall. It is said that around the year 1655 Edward Tyldesley, a member of a Catholic pro-Royalist family, whose seat was at Myerscough Hall, near Garstang, built Fox Hall as a summer residence. An alternative theory is that given the Hall's remote location, it was, in fact, used as a base for pro-Royalist activities, and that Charles II may well have been a regular visitor in the years before the Restoration. The Hall was close enough to the sea to allow the King a chance of escape should the need arise. Fox Hall was eventually abandoned by the Tyldesleys and, after being used as a farm, was converted into an inn; alas, nothing remains of the original building.

In 1751, Blackpool as a town in its own right appears on a map, thanks to the cartographer Emmanuel Bowen who recorded the place as Black Pool Town. There wasn't much to see, perhaps twenty or thirty cottages, but it was a start, and the craze for sea-bathing was gaining momentum. By the end of the 1750s Black Pool Town consisted of cottages, the Gynn Inn, two hotels and Fox Hall. It was in the 1780s that the area became a fashionable haunt for the sea-bathing set. In 1784 a summer season coach service operated from the Lower Swan Inn, Manchester, every Monday, Wednesday and Friday. The journey took about twelve hours; the inside fare was 14s, and a meal stop was made at the Black Bull Inn, Preston. Most of the inhabitants, however, continued to earn their living either labouring on the land, or fishing, or both.

One story about the village goes back to the year 1799 when the Lancashire potato crop failed, and the corn harvest was so poor that prices rocketed. On top of this, a freak storm broke along the coast, wrecking fishing boats, flooding inland and destroying or damaging many of the cottages. The people of Blackpool were now facing winter with little or no food reserves, and were unable to meet the prices being demanded inland. But salvation comes in many forms. As the storm destroyed their homes and livelihoods, it also carried with it a merchantship, sails torn away and rudder smashed. Despite their own suffering, men made their way down to the beach to try and help the crew of the stricken ship, which by now was aground and in danger of breaking up. Then from nowhere a giant wave lifted the vessel bodily and brought it further up the beach, enabling the crew to be rescued before she broke up. Amid the debris were barrels, sacks and packages. It turned out that her cargo was mainly provisions, the bulk of it peas. The people of Blackpool survived the winter of 1799-1800 on a diet of peas, fish and cockles.

By the time the railway arrived in Blackpool in 1846, the town was already a resort attracting several thousand visitors a year. Baileys Hotel, later the Metropole, had opened in 1776. The first bathing-machines had been imported by an enterprising inn keeper as early as 1730, though whether or not they were available for hire on Sundays, as the two machines at Lytham were, so that the frail could be trundled to and from church, is unknown. One of the earliest attractions was Uncle Tom's Cabin, which started out as little more than a wooden hut from which Thomas Parkinson sold sweetmeats and ginger beer during the summer season. Parkinson appears to have gone under the name of 'Uncle Tom', hence the name of Uncle Tom's Cabin.

Eventually Parkinson sold out to a man named Taylor. He went into partnership with another man in order to develop the business, but they did turn down the chance to buy the field the cabin stood in, and the one next to it, for just £15. Fate now plays its hand. Some time after Taylor had taken over, a wooden bust of a negro, thought to be a ship's figurehead, was washed ashore. By coincidence, one of the best-selling books of the time was 'Uncle Tom's Cabin', so Taylor simply stuck the figurehead on the roof, and added those of Eva and Topsy, implying that the cabin was in fact named after the hero of the book.

THE PARADE FROM THE TOWER
1896 / 38859

During the 1830s Blackpool was still developing along genteel lines, though it must be said that for several decades the tradition of the Lancashire working people and their families visiting the town had already begun, albeit on a small scale. Many would make the journey by cart; some would even walk, just to spend a few hours away from the dust, grit, grime and monotony of mill and factory life. Some resorts simply didn't want the lower social orders at play; the Yorkshire spa Scarborough even issued a broadsheet stating that 'the watering place has no wish for a greater influx of vagrants and those who have no money to spend'. The Scarborough broadsheet was also an attack on the railways, the very mode of transport that would bring both it, and the likes of Blackpool and Southport, much of their wealth.

VICTORIAN DEVELOPMENT

By the 1870s many Lancashire cotton workers were enjoying the luxury of three unpaid days' holiday a year, which when tacked onto a weekend gave a handy five-day break. Another important development for Blackpool's holiday industry was the passing of the Bank Holidays Act in 1871. With specific days allocated for holidays, the railway companies could schedule special excursion trains knowing that they would be filled. With the railway, investment in Blackpool's infrastructure and attractions gathered momentum. The North Pier opened in 1863 and was followed by a second, the South Jetty, in 1868. In 1879 electric lighting was introduced along the promenade and the first illuminated tramcars ran as early as 1897, inspired, it is said, by the Kaiser's birthday celebrations in Berlin.

While Scarborough, Southport and Morecambe continued to provide for the genteel classes, Blackpool was developing along more gregarious lines. When they were opened in 1878, the Winter Gardens were probably the town's last throw at catering for a sophisticated audience. They housed a library, reading room, art gallery and concert hall. But the writing was on the wall as early as Whit weekend 1879, when the Garden's principal attraction was a young lady being fired from a cannon. As the popularity of the Gardens grew, so Uncle Tom's Cabin declined, despite the fact that it too had its own dance

9

orchestra. For Uncle Tom's the end would come in 1906; not the victim of financial circumstances, but of nature itself, when cliff erosion caused a part of the buildings to collapse.

In September 1885, Blackpool opened the first fare-paying street-tramway in the country to be equipped with electric cars. Initially the tramway was confined to the promenade, where it ran over a two-mile single line, with passing loops every three hundred yards. The trams were powered by what was known as the conduit system, a positive current being carried by copper conductors in a central channel between the tracks. The cars were fitted with a shoe, which fitted into the conduit and made contact with the conductors, thereby picking up the current. The cars were capable of speeds in excess of 15mph, but were, in fact, restricted by an interfering Board of Trade to 8mph. Though successful, the system had its drawbacks in that the conduit was prone to loss of current due to its filling with sea water or drifting sand. The Corporation took over the line in 1892 and converted it to overhead wire in 1898-99.

In 1894 Blackpool pulled off the seaside coup of the century with the opening of the Tower. Blackpool has never been shy of borrowing good ideas from elsewhere. At 518ft high, the Tower was based on that in Paris. As the crowds

CENTRAL PIER
1906 / 53855

flocked in to see this engineering masterpiece, other resorts announced their intentions to build their own towers; but only Morecambe and New Brighton ever got anywhere. The Tower was followed in 1899 with the opening of the Tower Ballroom, modelled on the Paris Opera House, and famed for its mighty Wurlitzer organ which would feature in countless BBC broadcasts and make organist Reginald Dixon a household name.

By the beginning of the 20th century Blackpool was the preferred holiday destination for the majority of Lancashire cotton workers, but it was also drawing in holiday-makers from as far afield as Scotland, the Midlands and the North East. During Wakes Week, 1919, no less than 10,000 people from Nelson stayed in Blackpool, while just 1,000 headed off to Southport and around 500 went to the Isle of Man, via Fleetwood. The town became adept at handling large influxes of people. On Bank Holiday Monday in August 1937, no less than 425 special trains ran to Blackpool and, over the bank holiday period, the town is said to have had five million visitors. True or not, we do know that on one day in July 1945 over 100,000 people came to the town by train.

The 1920 Dunlop Guide describes Blackpool as 'the most popular seaside resort in England: scene of the holiday revels of Manchester, Liverpool, and the industrial centres of Lancashire generally. Blackpool has gone into the 'business' of catering for the millions exactly as into a business, and it was the pioneer in the advertising of local attractions, having secured a local Act of Parliament authorising expenditure out of the rates for that purpose. It is a frankly democratic and by no means exclusive place, but the entertainments, of which there is an almost endless variety, are the very best of their kind. The theatres, concert halls, zoological gardens, dancing saloons or ballrooms, gardens, Eiffel Tower, and other ingenious attractions are maintained with the most lavish expenditure of money. The site of Blackpool, a little over a century ago, was a sandy waste, and the town is scarce half-a-century old'.

While Blackpool followed the pack-them-in-and-give-them-what-they-want road, Lytham St Annes and Southport became popular residential areas for Lancashire businessmen. It allowed them to appear prosperous, as indeed many of them were, without overdoing it. In B Bowker's book 'Lancashire under the Hammer', he relates the story of a weaver who married his boss's daughter in 1908 and went to work at the Manchester Exchange, where he sold yarn on a fixed commission rate of half a per cent. Within four years the ex-weaver had made enough money to buy a house in Southport. By 1920 he had made over £150,000 and had moved into a large house at St Annes. Lytham's development was due to the influence of the Clifton family, who owned more than 15,000 acres in southwest Lancashire; most of it was acquired at the time of the Dissolution. St Annes was to be the last of the Fylde resorts to be developed, and would eventually be joined to Lytham.

THE GOLDEN MILE

Eager for new attractions guaranteed to pull in the crowds, the Corporation organized an Aviation Week in October 1909. What we have to remember in 1999 is that ninety years ago, flying was an 'in' thing. In 1909 Louis Bleriot caused a sensation when he successfully flew across the English Channel, and the aviators of his day were idolized, much the same as rock and film stars are today. Thousands came to Blackpool to watch pilots and aircraft compete in races for prize money ranging from £50 to £2,000. The event was repeated in 1910. When Graham White landed his plane on the beach near the Victoria Pier, hundreds of spectators scrambled for a chance to touch the machine. Thousands watched from the beach and the Golden Mile as a French aviator flew around and over the Tower, and another pilot broke the world height record by flying at more than one mile high.

In 1910 the Corporation evicted a gipsy camp on the South Shore, as the site was being redeveloped as the Pleasure Beach. As early as 1907 Blackpool had opened a scenic railway, the first of its type in the UK, though already popular in amusement parks in the United States. The Casino opened in 1913 and included a restaurant, cinema and billiard hall, and when the Big Dipper was built in 1923 at a cost of £25,000 it set in motion the trend by which the Pleasure Beach Company continues to invest in new and exciting rides.

As early as 1919, the Golden Mile was awash with sideshows and paper hats bearing that well-known legend 'Kiss Me Quick'. It was all a part of the atmosphere, bordering on the naughty, but not quite getting there. In the late 1930s Blackpool's reputation as an 'anything goes' place was the subject of a Mass Observation survey after seventy-six babies were born in the town out of wedlock in 1936. But of the 400 or so couples caught in the middle of the night on the beach, or under the piers, only four couples were engaged in anything other than holding hands or kissing. Of the four couples, one included a member of the Mass Observation, who was obviously doing his bit to bump up the statistics!

Blackpool's reputation was due mainly to the likes of showmen like Luke Gannon, who would try almost anything once. In the 1930s Luke Gannon offered the Reverend Harold Davidson, the defrocked Rector of Stiffkey, £100 a week to live in a barrel on the Golden Mile. The Rector had been thrown out of the Church for ministering unto young ladies in ways other than spiritual. His defence was made all the harder when the prosecution got its hands on several pictures of Davidson cavorting naked with the ladies in question.

FLEETWOOD
THE HARBOUR 1894 / 33968

Sandwiched between a fasting girl and a flea circus, Davidson sat in his barrel expounding on the injustice of his situation. In August 1938, Davidson's final demonstration of his innocence was to appear at Skegness among the lions of a travelling menagerie. He was a sort of latter-day Daniel in the lions' den—but a lion ate him. Hundreds attended his funeral and fought one another for handfuls of earth from his grave.

During the summer of 1938, Gannon had the punters paying 2d a time to see the newly wedded Colonel and Mrs Barker lying in separate beds, their marriage as yet unconsummated. The Colonel was supposed to have been born a woman, and had undergone the world's first sex change operation to become a fully functioning male. The reason the two were lying there was said to be for a bet; the Colonel stood to win £250 if he could keep his new-found manhood to himself for twenty-one weeks. It was all a con. At night, when our love-sick couple were supposedly being monitored by Gannon's ever vigilant staff, the Colonel, who was a man, was at home with his mistress, while his 'wife' went off to her digs.

Blackpool continues to attract large numbers of visitors, despite the competition from package holidays and last-minute deals by travel agents. The Pleasure Gardens prides itself on its spectacular rides, and seems to be locked in some kind of duel with Alton Towers to come up with the most hair-raising. The trams continue to run, and the Tower is still standing; other places would have almost certainly got rid of both of them in the so-called name of progress. If you have never been to Blackpool, don't knock it until you have tried it.

FLEETWOOD

Fleetwood was founded in 1836 by Sir Peter Hesketh-Fleetwood, and was laid out to the designs of Decimus Burton, who designed the North Euston Hotel, Queen's Terrace and both lighthouses.

They planned that the town would be a little way inland and separate from the dock area. For a short time Fleetwood was, in effect, the northern terminus of the London & North Western Railway line from Euston, and the connecting stop for steamer services to and from Belfast, Ardrossan and various west coast ports. The railway reached Fleetwood in July 1840, six years before it reached Blackpool.

The line was a single track and ran from Preston via Kirkham, Poulton and Thornton. Fleetwood lacked the infrastructure to compete with Liverpool as a major port for passenger and cargo traffic, but it did become England's principal fishing port on the west coast, with a fleet to rival those of Hull and Grimsby. The advantage that Fleetwood had as a port was that its entrance channel was free of hazards to navigation such as sandbars and moving banks. Even at low tide, vessels drawing less than sixteen feet of water could manoeuvre within the harbour basin, and boats drawing less than five feet could still use the channel.

A 1906 tour guide describes Fleetwood as,'a flourishing watering-place on the Irish Channel. Mail steamers ply hence daily to Belfast, and there is a summer-service to the Isle of Man. About 3m to the S.W. is Rossall School, a large public school (400 boys)'. Rossall Hall had been the home of Sir Hesketh-Fleetwood, and became a school in 1844.

LYTHAM & ST ANNE'S
Lytham was to develop on somewhat more genteel lines than Blackpool, owing to the influence of the Clifton family who owned over 15,000 acres in southwest Lancashire. Their land in Lytham had been acquired at the time of the Dissolution when they purchased the estates of the former Benedictine priory.

There were two bathing machines at Lytham by the mid-1730s. The added bonus was that they were available for hire on Sundays, so that those of a more frail disposition might be trundled to church and back. St Anne's was the last of the Fylde resorts to be developed, and though it would eventually join with Lytham to form the Borough of Lytham St Anne's, it was originally a separate Urban District. The town was laid out in the garden city fashion and, as in Lytham and Southport, merchants, mill owners and manufacturers soon took up residence.

In its heyday, Uncle Tom's Cabin offered dancing to its own orchestra, refreshments, and American Portraits 'taken and finished while you wait'. On the roof are three wooden figures representing Uncle Tom, Eva and Topsy. Shortly after this picture was taken in 1906, cliff erosion caused a part of the building to collapse; the remainder was demolished in 1907.

UNCLE TOM'S CABIN
1906 / 53875

NORTH PROMENADE

1906 / 53874

A Dreadnought tramcar approaches the terminus at Queen's Gate. At this time the Blackpool and Fleetwood tramway systems were separate concerns, and even lacked a connecting line. Those wishing to continue north had to walk a few yards to the Fleetwood terminus and join a tram there.

The cliff walk along the North Shore. The walk features heavily in the annual illuminations; many of the set pieces are erected along it.

NORTH SHORE
C1955 / B116014

The cliff walk and the Gynn tram stop. The Gynn was
a busy junction in the heyday of the tramway system.
There was a line from here to the North Station, and
it was also here that the trams belonging to Lytham St
Anne's Corporation terminated.

CLIFF WALK, NORTH SHORE
c1955 / B116022

NORTH SHORE
1890 / 22886

Bathing machines await customers. A typical machine had a door and a pair of shafts at either end. The lady would enter from the landward side, whilst the horse was attached to the seaward end. Once in the water, the lady, suitably attired to protect her modesty, would leave the machine and bathe.

The hydropathic craze swept Britain from the 1840s onwards, when a German practitioner named Vincenz Priessnitz developed a series of treatments using ordinary cold water, thus saving the need to visit a spa town. There were dozens of treatments, some including the use of electricity.

THE IMPERIAL HYDROPATHIC ESTABLISHMENT

1890 / 22890

This view also shows the Imperial Hydropathic Hotel. Hydros were for the more affluent visitor, charging anything between 8s 6d and 10s 6d per day, with treatments extra. Among the facilities at places like the Norbeck Hall Hydro were tennis courts and an indoor swimming pool.

CLAREMONT PARK TERRACE
1890 / 22889

I DO LIKE TO STROLL ALONG THE PROM...

The North Promenade offered walkways on different levels. Here residents from the hydropathic establishments could avail themselves of a pre-dinner constitutional and take in the bracing sea air. The hydropathic regime consisted of exercise, water treatments and regulated diets; hydros weren't too keen on alcohol either.

NORTH
PROMENADE
1906 / 53873

Is this family smiling for the camera, or have they noticed that little Johnny, head down and pedalling like mad, is on a collision course with our man from Frith? Apart from that, notice the old cottage between the two terraces.

THE TERRACE

1890 / 22887

TALBOT SQUARE

1890 / 22893

On the left is the ornate drinking fountain, while over on the right is one of the town's earliest theatres, the Theatre Royal, which opened in 1868. Talbot Road was developed by Thomas Clifton to link his estate at Layton with the Promenade. When he died, Thomas bequeathed Talbot Square to the town.

This view is taken from Talbot Square. The oldest of the town's three piers, this one dates from 1863, and when it opened was known simply as Blackpool Pier. By that time, Blackpool's nearby rival Southport had had a pier for three years; it was 1,200 yards long and capable of handling excursion steamers.

NORTH PIER AND FOUNTAIN
1890 / 22879

The departure of an excursion steamer attracts the attention
of several promenaders. At this time the longest pier in the
country was at Southport, but in 1897 it was eclipsed by
the pier at Southend.

NORTH PIER
1890 / 22880

A view from the North Pier towards Talbot Square. On the right is the 100-bed Clifton Hotel, an extensively rebuilt inn, originally named the Clifton Arms in honour of Thomas Clifton.

THE CLIFTON HOTEL FROM THE PIER
1890 / 22878

Visitors are out for an afternoon stroll. Notice just how immaculate the pier is: but then this was in the days before ice-cream wrappers, cola and lager cans, crisp packets, and chewing gum.

ON THE NORTH PIER
1890 / 22877

It's 'on with the show' on the North Pier with an afternoon concert.
Among the popular seaside entertainments were minstrel shows,
which had originated in the USA in the early nineteenth century.
The entertainers usually, but not necessarily, wore blackface makeup,
sang songs and told jokes.

FROM NORTH PIER
1899 / 43330

There is a bit of a swell on, and the majority of people are wrapped up warmly. The picture gives us an indication of the size of the Gigantic Wheel at the Winter Gardens and the imposing bulk of the Tower.

FROM THE PIER
1896 / 38839

This photograph gives us a good view of the new sea wall built as part of the widening of the Promenade. In 1910, the section from North Pier round the Metropole to Cocker Street was widened; the work was completed in time for Easter 1911. The in-fill was sand, brought from the southern end of town by means of a specially laid railway line.

FROM NORTH PIER
1906 / 53852

Built in 1776, the building has been enlarged and extended, and is now a part of the Metropole Hotel. It is still possible to make out a part of the building shown here by standing on the North Pier and looking at the near left-hand side and corner of the Metropole.

BAILEYS HOTEL
1895 / 35578

Sail boats and bathing machines dominate the beach area between the North Pier and the South Jetty. In the distance we get some idea of the development of this end of the town.

FROM THE SOUTH JETTY
1890 / 22867

A pre-Tower picture. Featured here are Dr W H Cocker's aquarium, menagerie and aviary, which occupied the site where the Tower now stands. The menagerie was retained as a Tower attraction, but it also gained fame as the setting for Stanley Holloway's monologue about young Albert Ramsbottom and the 'to do' when Albert was eaten by the menagerie lion.

THE AQUARIUM
1890 / 22888

The sea front on a somewhat stormy day. In the centre of the picture is the Prince of Wales Theatre, one of three in the town. One of the earliest was the Borough Theatre and Concert Hall, which later became Bannisters Arcade. After a second spell as a theatre, it became the local branch of C & A.

FROM THE PIER
1891 / 29597

From the same sequence as the previous storm picture, it is not too difficult to understand the operating problems the corporation experienced with its first trams, due to sea water and drifting sand getting into the conduit power supply. It was for these reasons that the system was converted to overhead power from June 1899.

THE SEA FRONT
1891 / 29594

There is not much of a chance for a donkey ride on a day like this one. This photograph was taken from somewhere near the entrance to the Central Pier. The tram lines are somewhere under the water.

THE TOWER
1896 / 38852A

THE TOWER FROM THE SANDS
1894 / 34802

The reflections of the Tower and the sailing boats kiss the sea on a brilliantly sunny, flat-calm day. The picture was taken from the Central Pier, and contrasts wonderfully with the grey skies and high sea in the picture on page 42. Given their numbering in the archive, it is possible that these pictures were taken within hours of one another.

FROM CENTRAL PIER
1896 / 38844

The most visitors to arrive on one day by train occurred in July 1945. With travel restrictions lifted, no less than 102,889 trippers passed through the town's three railway stations. No one knows how many others came by car, bus or motorcycle.

CENTRAL PROMENADE

c1955 / B116017

FROM CENTRAL PIER

1899 / 43333

THE TOWER AND CENTRAL PROMENADE

c1955 / B116021

Despite the grand appearance of the building, the acoustics in the Winter Gardens pavilion were suspect. When Sarah Bernhardt was engaged to play the female lead in 'The Lady of the Camellias', she had so much difficulty in making herself heard that she walked out at the end of the first act and never went back.

THE WINTER GARDENS
1894 / 33954

The Palatine Hotel was one of the largest in the resort with 120 beds, though the Metropole and the hydropathic establishments were bigger. The County, Clifton, and Palatine were in a similar price range, and in 1906 their daily pension rate (room, meals and all services) was 8s 6d a day.

THE PALATINE HOTEL
1890 / 22891

Built next to the Winter Gardens in 1896 in an attempt to compete with the Tower, the 220ft Gigantic Wheel was a financial disaster. The ride cost 6d and lasted for one complete revolution of the wheel. However, every time one of the cars reached the bottom the wheel was stopped while it was unloaded and reloaded.

THE BIG WHEEL
1896 / 38865

THE BIG WHEEL
1896 / 38867

Fancy a thing like this at the bottom of the garden?
Each of the thirty cars held thirty passengers, and the
ride lasted for about fifteen minutes. Losses were so great
that as early as 1901 the Gardens seriously considered
dismantling the brute, and were only stopped from doing
so because the costs would prove prohibitive.

This photograph includes the Winter Gardens in the background. In 1887, William Holland was appointed manager. Holland had worked in the rough and tumble of the London music hall business, and his philosophy was simple: to give holiday makers the sort of entertainments they wanted, no matter how crass.

ABINGDON STREET
1890 / 22894

James Duckworth Ltd, the grocery and provision chain, had a branch in this street, and others in Waterloo Road and Whitegate Drive. It was possible to place a grocery order at your local Duckworth branch, who would then arrange for one of the Blackpool shops to deliver it to your holiday accommodation in time for your arrival.

CHURCH STREET
1901 / 47039

Most of the Wakes Week holiday-makers provided their own food, which was then cooked for them by the landlady; each room would have its own food locker in the dining room. There were plenty of inexpensive boarding houses charging only a shilling or two per night.

DEAN STREET
1901 / 47040

THE NURSES' HOME
1899 / 43480

This is the nurses' home at the local hospital. Nurses were unmarried and there were strict regulations governing their behaviour, both on and off duty. Gentlemen callers were not allowed beyond the foyer, under any circumstances whatsoever. Some nurses' homes even had resort to wrapping barbed wire around drainpipes.

CHRIST CHURCH
1890 / 22899

This shows the new pavilion on the Central Pier. It is hard to believe that when this pier was built, it was so far away from the town centre that the revenue it generated fell far short of what had been anticipated. To boost business, the pier operated excursions by steamer to Southport.

CENTRAL PIER
1906 / 53855

As with many seaside resorts, one of the popular attractions was a trip in a boat. At Blackpool, sailing boats were often loaded and unloaded by means of portable gangways, one of which is in the picture. In the background is the North Pier, with an excursion steamer alongside its landing stage. This picture was taken from the South Jetty.

FROM SOUTH JETTY
1890 / 22868

As well as portable gangways, boat-carts were also used to get trippers to and from the sailing boats. In this picture, a boat-cart awaits the call to action, while the bathing machine concession has at least one paying customer in the water.

CENTRAL BEACH
1890 / 22870

The tide is in, the sea is calm and the bathing machines have nowhere to go except on the Promenade. This picture was taken from the Central Pier and gives us an idea of what the town's sea defences looked like prior to the widening of the Promenade and the construction of the sea wall we all know and love today.

CENTRAL PIER

1896 / 38852

A Dreadnought supertram rattles along the Promenade. These trams were capable of carrying 100 passengers; their unique design, with staircases either side of the driving positions, meant they could load and unload very quickly. During the season these trams operated with a crew of three: a driver and two conductors.

THE PROMENADE
1906 / 53869

By the mid-1890s, most Lancashire cotton towns enjoyed a full Wakes Week. Places such as Blackburn and Burnley were all but empty as millworkers and their families escaped en masse to Blackpool, Southport, Morecambe, Scarborough and North Wales.

VIEW FROM THE PALATINE HOTEL
1890 / 22874

VIEW FROM THE PALATINE HOTEL
1906 / 53849

The most striking difference between this and the previous picture is the widening of the Promenade. The basic idea was to build a new sea wall, and then to pack the gap between it and the old defences with sand; the surface was then paved over.

The early tramway system suffered from heavy voltage loss due to inadequate insulation. This restricted the number of trams able to operate at any given time, and one of the measures taken to prevent the system from overloading was the introduction of a flat rate fare of 2d. This effectively put the trams beyond the pocket of many visitors.

THE ELECTRIC RAILCAR
1890 / 22873

A wagonette loaded with holiday-makers stands near
Isaac Wilde's photography studio. Also in this block was
Holden's dining rooms, Wolstenholmes (photographer to
the Lord Mayor of London), Horace Fowler, who sold
only non-alcoholic beer and soft drinks, and a place
where you could hire tricycles.

FROM SOUTH PIER
1890 / 22872

The tide is well and truly out. In those days, the beach area would often be a hive of activity, including donkey rides, ice cream and sweet stalls, shell fish and oyster sellers.

THE SANDS
1896 / 38858

By the 1870s, many Lancashire cotton workers received three day's unpaid holiday a year, which was tacked onto a weekend to give a five-day break. Cheap rail fares and discounts at digs for block bookings boosted the holiday trade at both Blackpool and Southport.

THE ESPLANADE
1890 / 22871

Wilfred Pickles used to tell a story about a mother and her son at a guest house. He had a broad accent, which embarrassed his mum. The little lad opened his mouth, but his mother guessed what he wanted and whispered 'Go upstairs, love. You know where it is'. A few seconds later there was a loud 'Mum!' from upstairs. 'I can see t'Tower while I'm on t'closet!'

THE SEA FRONT
1901 / 47034

THE SEA FRONT

At the time when this picture was taken, a holiday in Blackpool represented a considerable outlay for the average factory or mill worker. There was no such thing as holiday pay, and wouldn't be until the 1930s. One way of saving was by making weekly payments into a holiday club.

The Pleasure Beach actually started as a fairground on the South Shore. One of the early rides was the Sir Hiram Maxim Flying Machine. The ride was built in 1904, and hurtled round at an exhilarating 40mph.

THE FLYING MACHINE
1906 / 53857

The Victoria Pier about a year after it had opened. A large pavilion was later built near the entrance to provide additional facilities, and the name was changed to the South Pier.

THE VICTORIA PIER
1894 / 33951

FROM
FLEETWOOD TO
QUEEN'S GATE

Pictured here is one of ten American-style, 48-seat enclosed cars supplied by Milnes & Co, which were fitted with controllers and motors supplied by General Electric of the USA.

FLEETWOOD
EAST STREET 1898 / 47074

Construction of the American-influenced Blackpool & Fleetwood Tramroad (B&FT) began in July 1897, and by September 1898 the line was fully opened. From Ash Street to the Blackpool terminus at Gynn, the tramroad ran on a reserved track segregated from other road traffic; it was only at the northern end that it actually ran through the streets of Fleetwood.

FLEETWOOD
EAST STREET 1898 / 41015

Over on the left is the Lancashire & Yorkshire and London & North Western joint railway station, which was conveniently built next to the steamer berths. On the right is one of the town's landmarks, the Pharos Lighthouse.

Fleetwood's other principal hotel was the Mount. The hotel was built with its front on the promenade, offering guests excellent views of the bay.

FLEETWOOD
THE MOUNT HOTEL 1901 / 47072

*The pier was considerably shorter
in length than those at Blackpool,
but somewhat similar in design to
the one at Aberystwyth.*

FLEETWOOD
THE PIER 1918 / 68413

The lower promenade, with the North Euston Hotel, owned by the London & North Western Railway, in the background. Also featured is the landing-stage for the ferry to Knott End-on-Sea.

FLEETWOOD
THE LOWER PROMENADE 1898 / 41009

Visit any resort where there are fishing vessels and you will be sure to find plenty of onlookers. In the distance is the landing stage at Knott End-on-Sea. For years, the service was worked by two boats, the 'Progress' and the 'Wyresdale'.

FLEETWOOD
THE FERRY 1901 / 47069

The turbine steamer 'Viking', departing for Douglas. When this picture was taken the turbine steamers were usually assigned to the Liverpool-Douglas and Heysham-Douglas services. It was also possible to sail to Douglas from Barrow, Silloth, Whitehaven and Glasgow.

Holiday-makers gather round one of the seaside entertainments. Unfortunately, we have no idea what they were watching, as the Frith cameraman didn't bother to record the details. It could be a Pierrot troupe, or even a minstrel show; both of these were popular acts at the time.

FLEETWOOD
THE BEACH 1902 / 49051

FLEETWOOD
'MONA'S QUEEN' 1904 / 52171

*The 'Mona's Queen', which belonged to the Isle of
Man Steam Packet Co, eases out of Fleetwood for a
summer sailing. The crossing to the Isle of Man took
about three hours; the daily sailing was scheduled to
leave after the arrival of the 2.15pm train. There was
also a twice-weekly sailing to Ramsey via Douglas.*

*The Furness Railway paddle-steamer 'Philomel' entering Fleetwood.
Built in 1899 for the General Steam Navigation Co, the paddler
was purchased by the Furness Railway in 1907. It entered service
on the Barrow-Fleetwood run in April 1908.*

FLEETWOOD
THE BARROW BOAT 1908 / 59940

It was here in 1847 that Queen Victoria first set foot in Lancashire, when she arrived at the harbour having travelled from Scotland by sea. The remainder of her journey was by train. Prince Albert had travelled by train in 1839, but it was not until 1842 that Victoria could be persuaded to take the train from Windsor to London.

FLEETWOOD
THE HARBOUR 1894 / 33968

Cleveleys is the most northerly, from Blackpool, of the small resorts leading up to Fleetwood. Though the resort was away from the railway, holiday-makers could easily reach it by tram, either from Fleetwood or from North Station. One of the earliest Corporation bus services was the Cleveleys to Thornton route, which began operating in July 1921.

CLEVELEYS
THE ARENA AND PROMENADE c1955 / C440009

Modern minstrel shows originated in the USA during the early 19th century, possibly the 1840s, with a troupe called the Christie Minstrels. The entertainers usually, but not necessarily, wore blackface makeup, sang songs and told jokes.

LYTHAM
'THE MINSTRELS' 1914 / 67479

Time for a donkey ride, sweets and ice cream. The summer of 1914 was long and hot; the hottest day of the year in Lancashire was 28 June.

LYTHAM

DONKEY RIDES 1914 / 67480

LYTHAM

At this time the resident population was around 9,000, compared to 58,000 for Blackpool. Even after amalgamating with St Anne's, the town continued to maintain its status as a quiet residential resort.

The town was well laid-out, and there were plenty of opulent villas available for those merchants and industrialists who preferred to live by the sea and commute.

LYTHAM

FROM THE PIER 1907 / 59120

Though well-maintained and kept in top-flight condition, Lytham Pier was of a somewhat functional design when compared to the one at St Anne's, or to the South Pier at Blackpool.

LYTHAM

THE PIER 1921 / 70740

The children's amusements at Lytham consisted of a few swings, donkey rides and a couple of stalls. There is quite a large crowd gathered down toward the old windmill. Unfortunately, we have no idea what is going on, but it is reasonable to assume that it is a concert.

LYTHAM

THE BEACH FROM THE PIER 1901 / 47085

The same view as the previous picture.
These two pictures give us some idea
of the different philosophies behind the
development of the Fylde resorts.

LYTHAM

FROM THE PIER 1894 / 33958

A Blackpool-bound tram pulls into the Market Square. Through-services to Blackpool began in 1897, and the route was via St Anne's, then along through the sand dunes of Clifton Drive, then to Squires Gate, and on to Station Road.

LYTHAM

MARKET SQUARE 1907 / 59131

LYTHAM

THE MARKET HALL AND FOUNTAIN 1890 / 22905

This classical-style brick building, with its heavy rustication, manages to look light-hearted, thanks to its cupola. It is a hot, sunny day and one of the tourists is putting up her parasol.

At this time the 20-bed Ship & Royal Hotel on Clifton Street (the telephone number was 186) was one of two Lytham hotels recommended by the AA. The other one was the Clifton Arms.

LYTHAM
CLIFTON STREET 1901 / 47082

The tramway was only electrified in 1903. Until then
it had operated using gas-propelled trams. The gas was
stored in reservoirs which gave sufficient fuel for sixteen
miles. The gas trams were far from satisfactory, with
the result that in 1900 twenty horse-trams were also
acquired.

LYTHAM

CLIFTON STREET 1907 / 59132

LYTHAM

CLIFTON STREET 1923 / 74193

On the right, Parkinson's shop is a typical grocer's shop in the old style, selling everything from tea to motor tours. Its frontage is smothered with famous old trade names including Cadburys, Lyons, St Bruno and St Julien.

There was a scheme to extend the tramway all the way to Preston via Freckleton. The only section to be built was a 1,100-yard single line from the terminus at Lytham to East Beach.

LYTHAM

CLIFTON STREET 1907 / 59133

This photograph looks towards the seafront and the pier. Though there are one or two motorcars around, the scene is relatively traffic free; people appear to be quite at ease either walking or standing in the middle of the road.

ST. ANNE'S

ST ANNE'S ROAD WEST 1913 / 66474

The other side of the street. The hardware store has had a pre-season facelift: a new awning, a coat of paint, and the relocation of the shop-sign from the ground to the second floor.

ST ANNE'S

ST ANNE'S ROAD WEST 1901 / 47091

Tramcar No 23 trundles along Clifton Drive South on its way to Lytham. The paving blocks between the tracks were made from white wood, balastic lava or jarrah. The running of connecting trams between Lytham and Blackpool began in 1905.

ST ANNE'S

CLIFTON DRIVE SOUTH 1914 / 67487

ST ANNE'S

THE BOAT TRIPS 1914 / 67490

Against a backdrop provided by the pier pavilion and landing stage, St Anne's boatmen are doing a brisk trade taking holiday-makers out for a trip around the bay. It is the long, hot summer of 1914 and, for young gentlemen, sailor's suits complete with silks and lanyards are the order of the day.

The Square has a French-sounding hairdresser's salon, a quality grocery store, and superbly-kept flower beds. The huge advertising signs above the grocer's and shoe shop would not be allowed today.

ST ANNE'S

THE SQUARE 1921 / 70745

The 1921 edition of the Dunlop book recommended three St Anne's hotels as being suitable for those on motoring holidays. There was the 260-bed Imperial Hydro (telephone, 258) with garage space for fifty automobiles, the Grand (telephone, 55) and the Station.

ST ANNE'S

THE BOATING POOL 1918 / 68340

ST ANNE'S

THE PIER 1906 / 53887

The design reflects a number of different styles: a mock-Tudor entrance, Chinese pavilions and an Indian-influenced palace. It must have looked superb when first opened.

Out for a stroll on a sunny summer afternoon. The pier is in immaculate condition, but then this is before the days of discarded ice cream wrappers, coke and beer cans, and anything else you care to think of.

ST ANNE'S
ON THE PIER 1906 / 53888

This exotic architectural confection reminds us of the Pavilion at Brighton, with its oriental domes and minarets. It must have seemed like something out of 'The Arabian Nights' to the average Victorian holidaymaker.

ST ANNE'S

THE PIER PAVILION 1906 / 53890

By 1921 the green fees at the Old Links, St Anne's were 2s 6d on weekdays and higher at weekends, whilst the Lytham & St Anne's club charged a fee of 5s for play on any day of the week.

ST ANNE'S

THE ROYAL LYTHAM GOLF CLUB HOUSE 1901 / 47106

At Fairhaven, visitors could take their exercise pulling on the oars of a rowing boat or playing 18 holes on the local golf course. Along with the Old Links and the Lytham & St Anne's, the Fairhaven was open to members of the Ladies' Golf Union. The Fairhaven was the only club on the Fylde coast that closed on Sundays.

FAIRHAVEN

THE LAKE 1923 / 74203

INDEX

FREE PRINT OF YOUR CHOICE

Choose any Frith photograph in this book.
Simply complete the Voucher opposite and
return it with your remittance for £2.25 (to
cover postage and handling) and we will print
the photograph of your choice in SEPIA (size
11 x 8 inches) and supply it in a cream mount
with a burgundy rule line
(overall size 14 x 11 inches).

**Please note: photographs with a reference number
starting with a "Z" are not Frith photographs and
cannot be supplied under this offer.**
Offer valid for delivery to UK one address only.

PLUS: **Order additional Mounted Prints at
HALF PRICE - £7.49 each** (normally £14.99)
If you would like to order more Frith prints
from this book, possibly as gifts for friends and
family, you can buy them at half price (with no
additional postage and handling costs).

PLUS: **Have your Mounted Prints framed**
For an extra £14.95 per print you can have your
mounted print(s) framed in an elegant polished
wood and gilt moulding, overall size
16 x 13 inches (no additional postage and
handling required).

Mounted Print
Overall size 14 x 11 inches (355 x 280mm)

IMPORTANT!

These special prices are only
available if you use this form to
order. You must use the ORIGINAL
VOUCHER (no copies permitted).

We can only despatch to one
UK address. This offer cannot be
combined with any other offer.

FRITH PRODUCTS AND SERVICES

All Frith photographs are available for you to buy as framed or mounted prints.
From time to time, other illustrated items such as Address Books and Maps are also
available. Already, almost 80,000 Frith archive photographs can be viewed and
purchased on the internet through the Frith website.

For more detailed information on Frith companies and products, visit:

www.francisfrith.co.uk

For further information, or trade enquiries, contact:
The Francis Frith Collection, Frith's Barn, Teffont, Salisbury SP3 5QP
Tel: +44 (0) 1722 716 376 Fax: +44 (0) 1722 716 881 Email: sales@francisfrith.co.uk